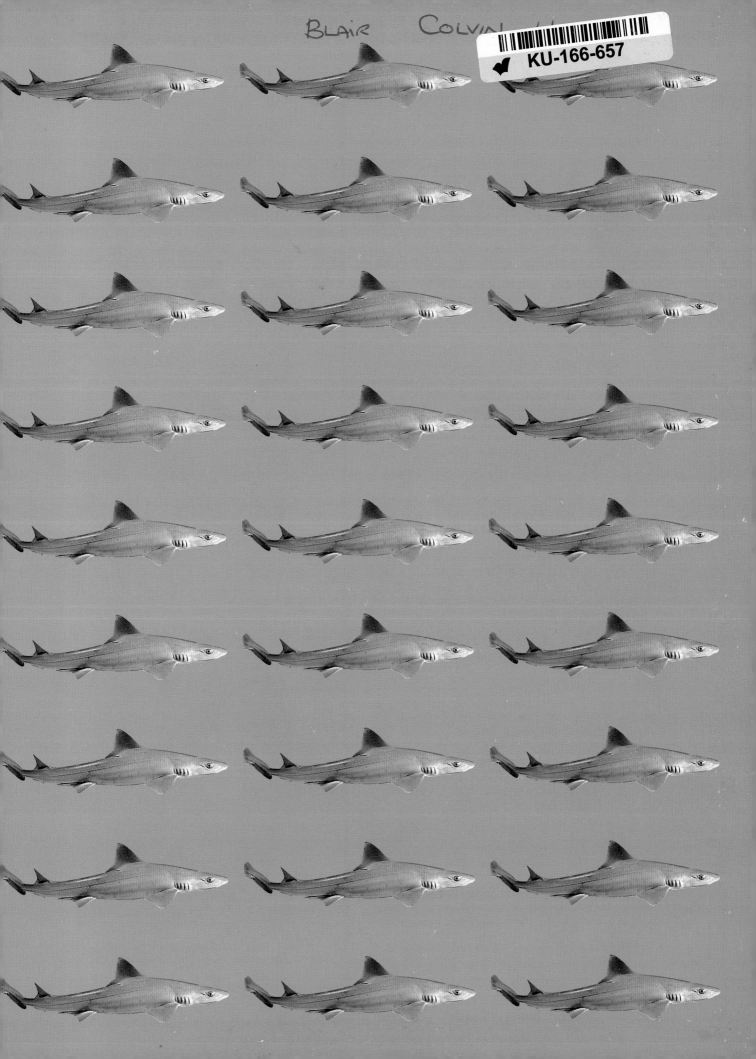

A DORLING KINDERSLEY BOOK

Project Editors Samantha Gray,
Patricia Grogan, Lee Simmons
Art Editors Penny Lamprell, Peter Radcliffe
Managing Editor Jane Yorke
Senior Art Editor Marcus James
Production Lisa Moss

Published in Great Britain by
Dorling Kindersley Limited,
9 Henrietta Street, London WC2E 8PS

2 4 6 8 10 9 7 5 3 1

ISBN 0-7513-5611-5

Colour reproduction by GRB, Italy
Printed in Belgium by Proost

Picture Agency credits The publisher would like to
thank the following for their kind permission to
reproduce the photographs: t=top, c=centre, b=bottom,
r=right, l=left, a=above.
The American Museum of Natural History, Library Services:
11cl; Natural History Picture Agency: Gerard Lacz 18bl, Henry
Ausloos 20ca; Planet Earth Pictures: 21clb, Pieter Folkens 7cr,
21ca; The Stock Market: 11bl; Jerry Young ©: 16tl stingray.

Photography by Andy Crawford, Mike Dunning, Neil
Fletcher, Frank Greenaway, Alan Hills, Dave King, Ray Moller,
Tracy Morgan, Steve Shott, Harry Taylor, Jerry Young.

Dorling Kindersley would like to thank Almudena Díaz for
DTP design, Mark Haygarth for jacket design, Tom Worsley
for picture research, and The Natural History Museum.

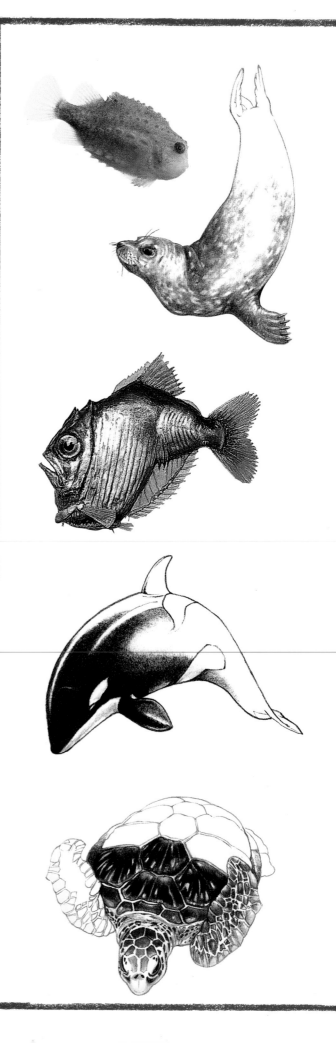

You·Can·Draw

SHARKS, WHALES, AND OTHER SEA CREATURES

Angelika Elsebach

Contents

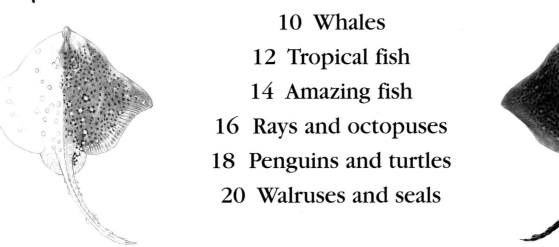

DORLING KINDERSLEY
London • New York • Moscow • Sydney

Introduction

This book shows you how to draw a range of fantastic sea creatures using a few easy techniques. First, look for the basic outline shape of the creature, and sketch this in. Then draw in internal shapes to create a more detailed body outline. Finally, add some guidelines so that you can position the creature's features. Finish off by colouring in your drawings.

Looking for outline shapes

It is easier to draw the outline of a sea creature if you divide it into one or more basic shapes in your imagination first.

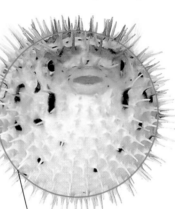

Basic outline shapes have been printed on photographs of sea creatures to help you.

Outline shapes can be drawn tilted at an angle.

The body of this swimming seal fits into a tall rectangle, and its head fits into a smaller one.

Checking proportion

To help you draw your sea creatures in proportion, use measurements of the size of the head and body to draw accurate outline shapes.

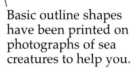

The body of a swimming ray forms a diamond shape.

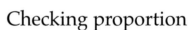

Look at the proportions of the body within each basic outline shape.

The head of this octopus fits into its total length one and a half times.

Drawing moving creatures

The bodies of sea creatures can look distorted as they swim, but look for the basic outline shape to help you draw your subject.

Sketching in a right-angled triangle makes it easier to draw a shark swimming towards you.

Perspective makes the body look narrower towards the tail.

This leopard shark fits into a basic oval shape as it turns.

Using guidelines
Look for internal shapes to help you draw a more realistic body outline, and add guidelines so that you can position the creature's features.

Internal shapes
Add internal shapes to create the basic body outline.

This shark's body is a tear-drop shape.

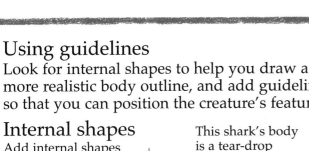

The basic outline is drawn in blue to help you see it.

Extending eye, nose, and mouth guidelines makes it easier to place other features.

Start to improve the outline.

Use crossing guidelines to position the eye and mouth.

Guidelines
Add blue guidelines to help position features such as eyes, mouth, and fins.

Improving outlines
Define the realistic outlines of the creature's head, body, and fins within the basic outline shape. Finally, add detail to the body and facial features.

Adding detail
Sea creatures often have intricate markings, so experiment with soft and hard pencils to colour in details of the creature you are drawing.

Use soft shading to show the seal's glistening, velvety fur.

Shading
Try using these techniques to create different effects.

Draw the outline of the markings on the shell before colouring them in.

Use a sharp, black pencil to draw the spiky whiskers.

Building up the colour in layers allows you to create areas of deep colour.

Graduate the shading on the flipper scales, and leave areas of paper to show through.

Shade in the face and flippers with a light base colour, then add the markings on top.

Use shading to show the cylindrical shape of the whale's body.

Shading with a soft pencil creates smudgy areas of shadow. Leave pale areas where light hits the body.

Define the rough shapes of the barnacles using a sharp, hard pencil.

Using a hard pencil to draw closely spaced, fine lines over shading suggests the texture of wrinkled skin.

Sharks

Here you can find out how to draw some amazing sharks. They come in a variety of stream-lined shapes, and they all have a distinctive dorsal fin.

The shark's fins are held straight out from its body.

Starry smooth-hound shark

Try drawing this shark from the side. Its body is a long, thin oval that tapers towards the tail.

Sketch in different-sized triangles for the fins.

1 First, draw the rectangular outline shape. Use guidelines to help you to position the internal shapes for the body, fins, and tail.

The tail is shaped like an upturned rectangle on a square.

The back of the dorsal fin curves inwards.

Use the horizontal guideline to position the eye.

2 Soften the outlines of the fins and tail. Draw a small circle for the eye and position the gills.

Add small, triangular fins near the tail.

Rub out the guidelines you don't need.

3 Use a sharp pencil to refine the outline of the shark. Add detail to the eye and gills.

Start to define the rounded shape of the body.

Use the side of a soft pencil to create light and dark areas of shading.

4 Shade in the body, allowing the paper to show through for the shiny areas of skin.

Shark's eye
Use a black pencil for the pupil. A white highlight makes the eye glint.

Graduate the shading to show the contours of the body.

Leopard shark

The leopard shark's stream-lined body forms an oval shape as it turns sharply.

The skin is covered in large spots.

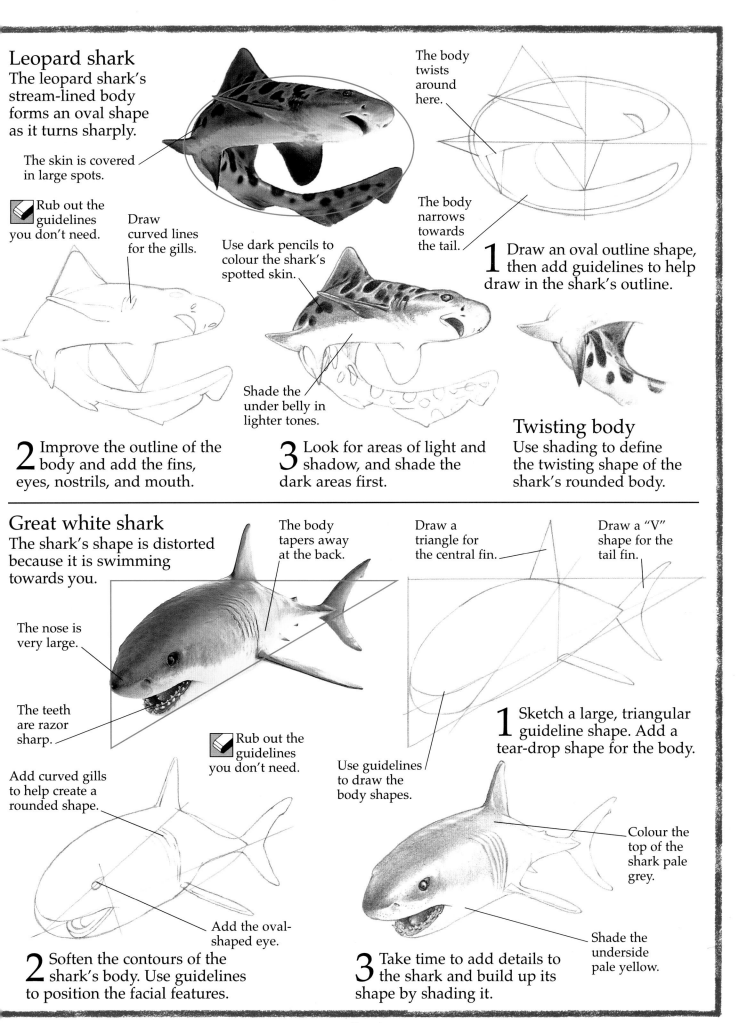

The body twists around here.

The body narrows towards the tail.

Rub out the guidelines you don't need.

Draw curved lines for the gills.

Use dark pencils to colour the shark's spotted skin.

Shade the under belly in lighter tones.

1 Draw an oval outline shape, then add guidelines to help draw in the shark's outline.

2 Improve the outline of the body and add the fins, eyes, nostrils, and mouth.

3 Look for areas of light and shadow, and shade the dark areas first.

Twisting body
Use shading to define the twisting shape of the shark's rounded body.

Great white shark

The shark's shape is distorted because it is swimming towards you.

The body tapers away at the back.

Draw a triangle for the central fin.

Draw a "V" shape for the tail fin.

The nose is very large.

The teeth are razor sharp.

Rub out the guidelines you don't need.

Use guidelines to draw the body shapes.

1 Sketch a large, triangular guideline shape. Add a tear-drop shape for the body.

Add curved gills to help create a rounded shape.

Add the oval-shaped eye.

Colour the top of the shark pale grey.

Shade the underside pale yellow.

2 Soften the contours of the shark's body. Use guidelines to position the facial features.

3 Take time to add details to the shark and build up its shape by shading it.

Whales

H ere you can find out how to draw a grey barnacled whale surfacing. The next page shows how to draw, colour, and add texture to a variety of other whales. Look for simple shapes to start your drawing.

Barnacled whale
This whale's large head and muscular body form a banana-shaped outline.

Draw a curved line to outline the head.

The whale has a long, cylindrical body.

The whale's tail forms a semicircle shape.

Sketch in a long triangle for the mouth.

The head is about one-quarter of the whale's total length.

Draw a soft oval shape for the flipper.

The body curves into the semicircular shape of the tail fin.

1 First draw the basic banana-shape outline. Add the internal shapes for the body, mouth, and flippers.

Barnacled skin
Use a hard, sharp pencil to define the outline of the barnacles scattered on the whale's body.

The eye sits at the end of the mouth line.

Rub out the guidelines you don't need.

Take time to define the details of the mouth and eye.

Draw barnacles all over the whale's skin.

Make the mouth curve, then add the teeth, and the hump on the head.

Make this side of the oval rounded.

Imagine the body is rounded like a cylinder as you colour it.

2 Sketch in the outline of the whale, softening the shapes of the body, mouth, and flippers.

3 Shade areas of shadow in dark grey. Let the paper show through on the light, shiny areas of skin.

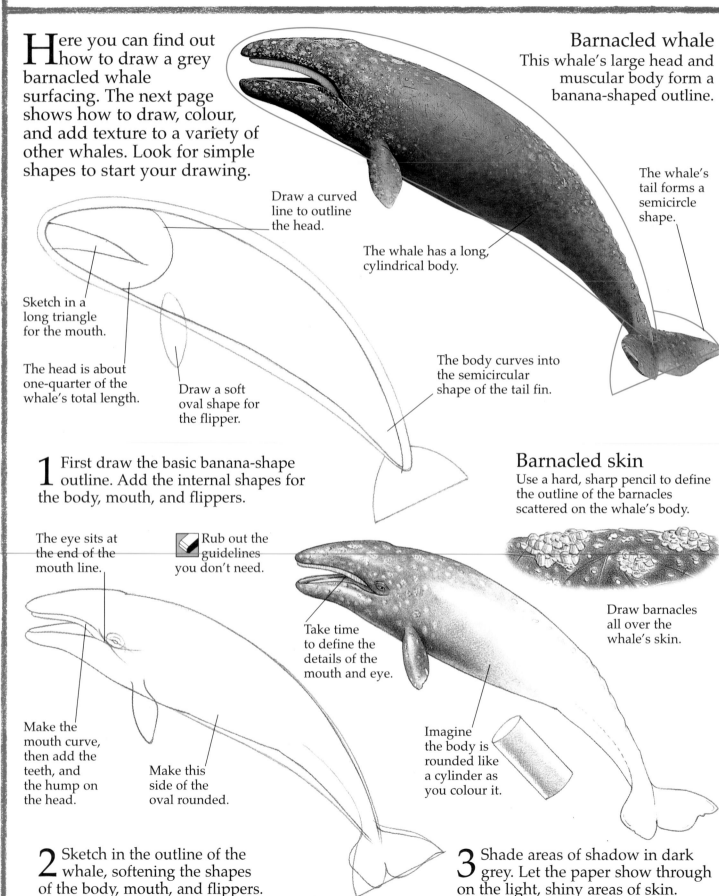

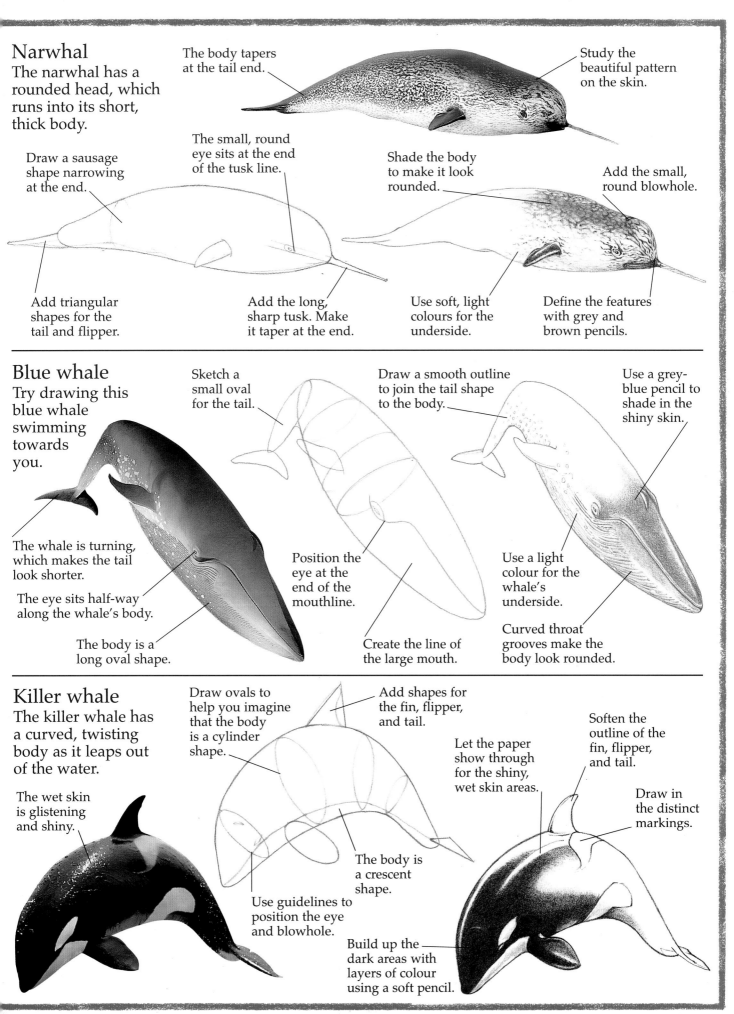

Narwhal

The narwhal has a rounded head, which runs into its short, thick body.

The body tapers at the tail end.

Study the beautiful pattern on the skin.

Draw a sausage shape narrowing at the end.

The small, round eye sits at the end of the tusk line.

Shade the body to make it look rounded.

Add the small, round blowhole.

Add triangular shapes for the tail and flipper.

Add the long, sharp tusk. Make it taper at the end.

Use soft, light colours for the underside.

Define the features with grey and brown pencils.

Blue whale

Try drawing this blue whale swimming towards you.

Sketch a small oval for the tail.

Draw a smooth outline to join the tail shape to the body.

Use a grey-blue pencil to shade in the shiny skin.

The whale is turning, which makes the tail look shorter.

The eye sits half-way along the whale's body.

The body is a long oval shape.

Position the eye at the end of the mouthline.

Create the line of the large mouth.

Use a light colour for the whale's underside.

Curved throat grooves make the body look rounded.

Killer whale

The killer whale has a curved, twisting body as it leaps out of the water.

Draw ovals to help you imagine that the body is a cylinder shape.

Add shapes for the fin, flipper, and tail.

Soften the outline of the fin, flipper, and tail.

The wet skin is glistening and shiny.

Let the paper show through for the shiny, wet skin areas.

Draw in the distinct markings.

The body is a crescent shape.

Use guidelines to position the eye and blowhole.

Build up the dark areas with layers of colour using a soft pencil.

11

Tropical fish

Tropical fish are very colourful and many have amazing, scaly patterns on their skin. Most are a basic oval shape. Here you can find out how to draw a clown triggerfish. On the next page you will find hints and tips on how to colour and shade other fish.

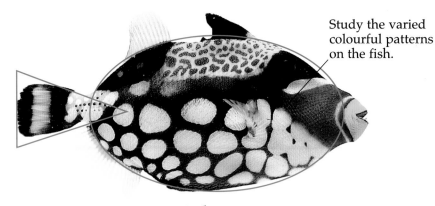

Study the varied colourful patterns on the fish.

Clown triggerfish
The dramatically patterned clown triggerfish has a rotund body.

The tail is about one-quarter of the fish's total length.

The top fins are further forward than the bottom fin.

Soften the shapes of the fins and tail.

Draw guidelines from the centre of the mouth.

Add an open mouth shape to the triangle.

1 Draw a basic oval shape for the body and simple shapes for the fins, mouth, and tail.

2 Use guidelines to position the eye and side fin. Sketch in a softer fish outline.

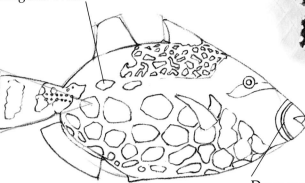

The main body pattern is a series of irregular ovals.

Rub out the guidelines you don't need.

Patterned scales
Draw fine, criss-cross lines to give the impression of scales, add the pattern, then colour them in.

Leave a curved white line to create depth.

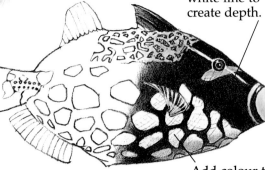

Draw curved markings around the mouth.

Add colour to the patterned scales.

3 Start adding surface detail. Draw in the shapes for the different skin patterns.

4 Shade in the main body colour, letting the paper shine through the lighter areas.

Clownfish

The clownfish has a simple, oval-shaped body with bold stripes and frill-like fins.

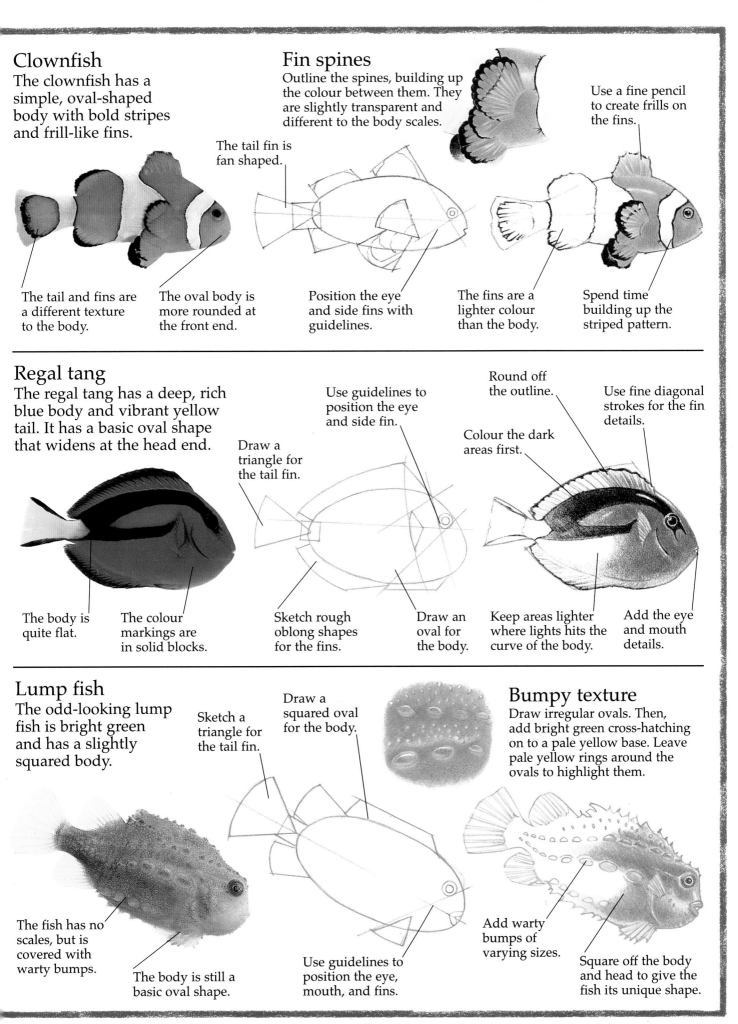

Fin spines

Outline the spines, building up the colour between them. They are slightly transparent and different to the body scales.

The tail fin is fan shaped.

Use a fine pencil to create frills on the fins.

The tail and fins are a different texture to the body.

The oval body is more rounded at the front end.

Position the eye and side fins with guidelines.

The fins are a lighter colour than the body.

Spend time building up the striped pattern.

Regal tang

The regal tang has a deep, rich blue body and vibrant yellow tail. It has a basic oval shape that widens at the head end.

Use guidelines to position the eye and side fin.

Round off the outline.

Use fine diagonal strokes for the fin details.

Draw a triangle for the tail fin.

Colour the dark areas first.

The body is quite flat.

The colour markings are in solid blocks.

Sketch rough oblong shapes for the fins.

Draw an oval for the body.

Keep areas lighter where lights hits the curve of the body.

Add the eye and mouth details.

Lump fish

The odd-looking lump fish is bright green and has a slightly squared body.

Sketch a triangle for the tail fin.

Draw a squared oval for the body.

Bumpy texture

Draw irregular ovals. Then, add bright green cross-hatching on to a pale yellow base. Leave pale yellow rings around the ovals to highlight them.

The fish has no scales, but is covered with warty bumps.

The body is still a basic oval shape.

Use guidelines to position the eye, mouth, and fins.

Add warty bumps of varying sizes.

Square off the body and head to give the fish its unique shape.

13

Amazing fish

The seas contain some fish that have rather unusual shapes. Here, you can find out how to draw the porcupine fish, which is completely round when inflated, but oval when deflated. On the next page you can learn how to draw two strange deep sea fish.

Porcupine fish
When scared or annoyed, the porcupine fish lifts its spines and puffs out like a ball.

Draw circular guidelines to help you position the spines.

The spines spiral out from the circular guidelines.

Draw long spines at the edges and short ones in the centre.

Divide the circle into sections with guidelines to position the eyes and mouth.

Add details to the eyes and mouth.

1 Draw a circle for the basic outline. Draw in the eyes, mouth, and fins.

Spines
Use a sharp pencil to draw diamond-shaped spines that are longer at one end.

2 Now, carefully add the spines all over the body. This will make the fish look rounded.

Rub out the guidelines you don't need.

Shade the fish a lighter colour at the bottom than at the top.

3 Colour the top part of the fish in a strong yellow and the bottom in a lighter yellow.

Deflated porcupine fish
Most of the time, the spines of the porcupine fish lie flat along its body.

Draw simple shapes for the tail, fins, and mouth.

Use guidelines to position the large eye and tail fins.

Shade in the spiny skin – the colour seems stronger than when inflated.

Add detail to the eye and open mouth.

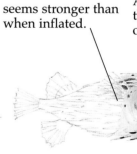

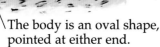
The body is an oval shape, pointed at either end.

The fish is quite flat.

Hatchet fish

The deep sea hatchet fish has a fairly complicated shape. Start by drawing a rectangle and triangle to help outline the body.

Ribbed skin

Use a fine, sharp pencil to define the ribbed skin, then shade it with the edge of a soft pencil.

The silvery body has a sharp-edged belly.

Draw triangles for the fins.

Soften and sketch in the outline of the body.

Take time to build up details on the spiny fins.

Divide the square into three to help you draw the basic outline of the fish.

Use guidelines to position the large eye.

Sketch angular shapes for different parts of the fish.

Draw in the characteristic ribbed lines on the body.

Gigantura

Gigantura has a long, narrow body, with bulging, binocular-like eyes. Its silvery body reflects light along its sides.

The shiny skin reflects light.

The fins point backwards.

Tubular eyeball

Sketch a short tube shape. Shade the top and bottom to create depth. Draw curved white lines to create a lens effect around the eyeball.

Sausage shaped body.

The long tail fin is covered in spines.

The top part of the tail fin is shorter than the lower part.

Draw basic shapes for the fins.

Sketch the eye.

Draw long straight lines for the tail fin.

Sketch a long, curved sausage shape for the body.

Colour the whole body in light grey then darken the top and bottom to create light and shadow.

Use guidelines to position the eye and tail fin.

Take time to build up the fin details.

Add sharp teeth.

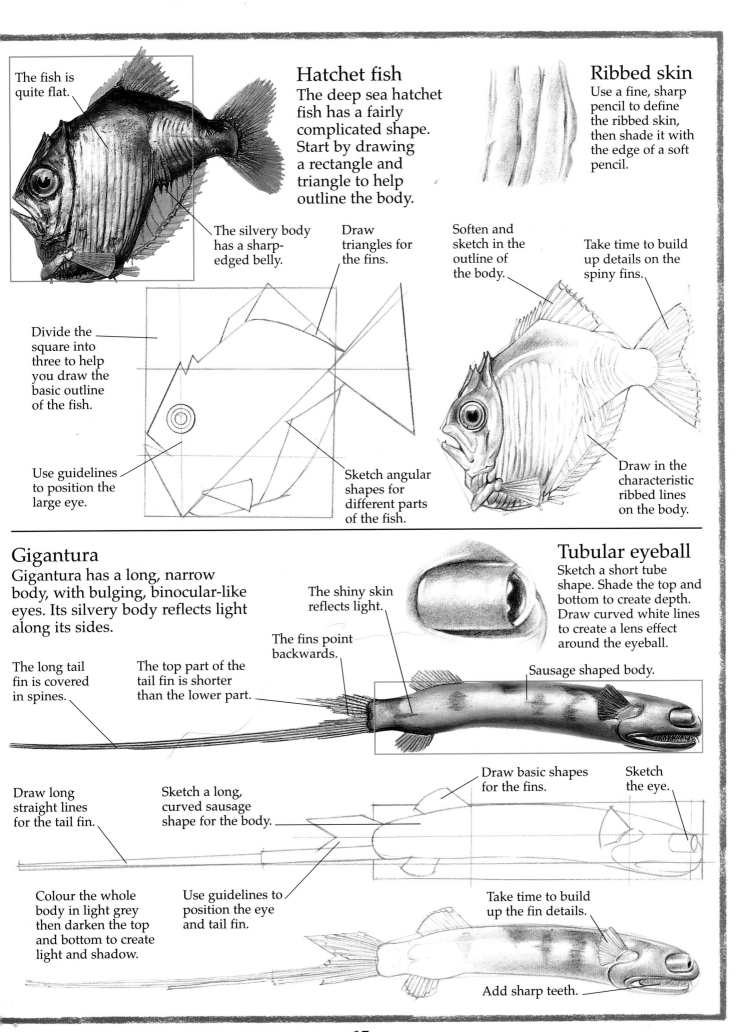

Rays

The seas contain many kinds of creature, including rays and octopuses. These pages show you how to draw a poisonous thornback ray and a common octopus.

Thornback ray

A thornback ray is a flat, diamond shape with a long tail. The tail has barbed thorns running down the sides.

The thornback ray is almost identical on each side of its spine.

1 Draw a diamond-shaped outline. Add curved guidelines to build up the fin shapes.

Add a guideline down the centre of the ray.

Add a curved guideline to help you draw the tail.

The nose sits at the tip of the diamond shape.

The eyes sit either side of the guidelines running from the nose.

The tail tapers towards the end.

Draw short lines close together to create the fins.

2 Draw more guidelines to help you position the eyes and nose. Start to improve the ray's outline.

Add barbed thorns to the tail.

Dappled skin

Use a soft pencil to shade the skin. Leave pale, circular patches to create the distinct spotty appearance.

3 Colour in the ray, filling in the details. Lay a darker colour on top of a lighter one to re-create the camouflage skin tones.

Swimming ray

The ray's body undulates as it swims along.

The tail is curved.

Sketch in the curved outline shape of the ray.

Add the dappled pattern on the skin.

Draw an angular, guideline shape.

The fins wave up and down.

Use guidelines to position the eyes, nose, and tail.

Colour in shadows where the fins curve.

Octopuses

Swimming octopus

A swimming common octopus forms a long, streamlined shape. The tentacles are close together.

Divide the rectangle into quarters to help position the octopus's tentacles.

The body fills almost half the rectangular guideline shape.

The common octopus has a dappled-orange topside, and a cream underside.

1 Draw an oval guideline shape for the head and a rectangle for the body. Sketch in the outline shapes.

Make the tentacles taper at the ends.

2 Use guidelines to help you draw the tentacles, position the eye, and add the mouth.

Add small semicircles for the suckers.

Outline the flowing shapes of the tentacles.

Use guidelines to help you position the eye.

Gently curve the end of the head.

3 Add the final details, then colour the whole octopus in a light, base colour. Add a darker colour to the topside.

Pale and creamy underside.

Let some areas of base colour show through to give a dappled look.

Use colour to define the top and bottom of the head.

Twisting octopus

This octopus has its tentacles splayed out and is twisting around.

Legs curl up at tips.

Suckers run along the underside of the legs.

Sketch an oval for the head and tiny circle for the eye.

Draw an irregular shape to help you position the body.

Add curved guidelines for the legs.

Twisting tentacles

Draw a line of suckers starting on one side of the tentacles and twisting over to the other side.

Shade the octopus a rich orange on the upperside.

Add a dark circle for the eye.

Draw round suckers on the legs.

17

Penguins

Here you can find out how to draw an emperor penguin standing and another penguin swimming. Start by using a few simple shapes to help you to position the body and features.

Emperor penguin
When standing, the penguin's body fits inside a tall rectangle.

Use guidelines to position the eye and beak.

Position the oval head on top of the rectangle.

The penguin's chest is covered in creamy white feathers.

1 Draw a long oval for the body and smaller ovals for the head, legs, and flippers. Add a triangular beak.

The flippers are long, pointed ovals that overlap the body.

The feet are rounded triangles.

2 Start to define the head and beak within the basic shapes.

The front of the body has a rounded shape.

Add detail to the feet.

3 Sketch in the body outline, and add the leg and flipper details.

Add the fluffy tail feathers.

Rub out the guidelines you don't need.

4 Shade in the dark areas, and use short, soft lines for the feathers.

The body feathers are tinged with yellow.

Sketch in the webbed area between the toes.

Swimming penguin
This penguin's long, oval body is more agile and streamlined in the water.

Draw an oval for the body and a small circle for the head.

Position features with guidelines.

Add long strokes to show the tail feathers.

Make soft, short strokes with a pencil to create the feathery texture of the penguin's body.

Turtles

Before you start drawing this green turtle swimming towards you, look at its body proportions. It has a large, circular body, a small, oval head, and kidney-shaped front flippers. The turtle also has two, smaller back flippers to help propel it along.

Green turtle
This turtle has a patterned shell and intricate markings on the face and flippers.

Flippers
Take time to draw the scales on the flippers. The shapes become larger towards the outer edges.

Add a guideline down the centre of the head and body.

1 Draw an outline square and sketch internal shapes for the head, body, and flippers.

The hexagonal shapes become smaller towards the back of the shell.

Draw guidelines to position the eyes.

Position the nostrils each side of the central line.

2 Divide up the shell with guidelines to help you to position the shell markings.

Rub out the guidelines you don't need.

The markings on the shell form rows of connecting hexagons.

Leave white highlights on the shell and scales.

3 Improve the body outline and shell pattern. Sketch in the flipper markings.

4 Colour in the patterns and define the back flippers. Shade in the areas of shadow.

Use a light colour on the face, then add the scaley pattern in a dark colour.

Walruses

The walrus is a huge animal with a head that is very small in relation to its body proportions. From the side, the walrus looks like a shapeless mass apart from its long, heavy tusks. It has a rough, wrinkled skin that hangs in folds over its body.

Side view of a walrus
Begin by looking at the shapes the walrus forms within a rectangle and a long, four-sided shape.

Draw a small circle for the head inside a large oval for the chest area.

1 Sketch in the internal body shapes. The walrus's chest is a large oval and the rest of the body can be divided into two circles.

2 Draw a rough outline for the body, and then sketch in basic shapes and lines for the flippers, face, and tusks.

Add guidelines to help you position the whiskers.

Rub out the guidelines you don't need.

Draw a smaller circle at the narrow end of the shape.

Draw in the long tusks.

Add short whiskers to the muzzle.

Use dark colours to shade in the shadowy areas of the body.

Tusks
Use a sharp pencil to draw the outline of the tusks, and vary the weight of the line.

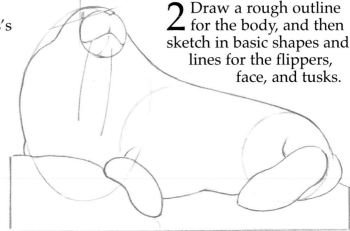

Take time adding details to the face.

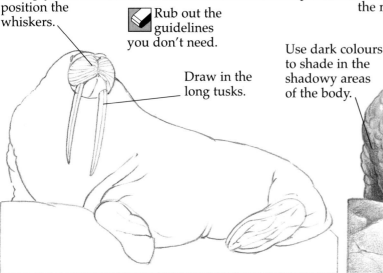

3 Improve the outline of your drawing and begin to add detail to the walrus's face, body, and flippers.

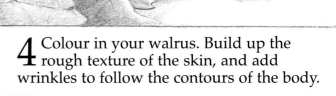

4 Colour in your walrus. Build up the rough texture of the skin, and add wrinkles to follow the contours of the body.

Seals

Seal's head

Try drawing a side-view of a seal's head. Use a square outline to help you form the shape of the head.

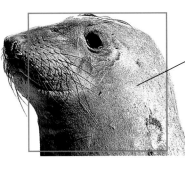

The seal has smooth, glistening fur.

The snout forms a short, pyramid shape.

Use guidelines to position the eye.

Draw in the shape of the nose and chin.

1 Draw in a circle for the head, and add a simple shape for the snout.

2 Sketch in the outline for the head, and use guidelines to position the facial features.

Whiskers

Use a sharp, dark pencil to draw whiskers that curl downwards.

Use a soft, smudgy pencil to shade in the dark areas.

Leave a white spot on the eye to make it glint.

Add a curved line for the mouth.

3 Lightly shade in the fur, and add detail to the eye, nose, and muzzle.

Swimming seal

Use simple outline shapes to draw a seal swimming. Its head and body fit into two, tilted rectangles.

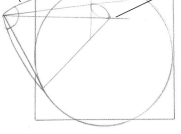
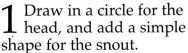

Crossing guidelines help to position the eye and muzzle.

2 Improve the outline of the head and body. Draw in guidelines to position the facial features.

1 Draw in a curved sausage shape for the body, and sketch in ovals for the head, chest, and back flippers.

Define the outline of the back flippers and tail.

Sketch in a small oval for the snout.

Add a simple shape for the tail.

Draw a basic kidney shape for the front flipper.

Add detail to the flippers.

Use a soft pencil to create the smudgy, dappled markings of the seal's wet fur.

Shade the neck area to emphasize the head twisting upwards.

Draw in the whiskers.

3 Shade the dark areas, and leave white highlights. Add detail to the eye, muzzle, and flippers.

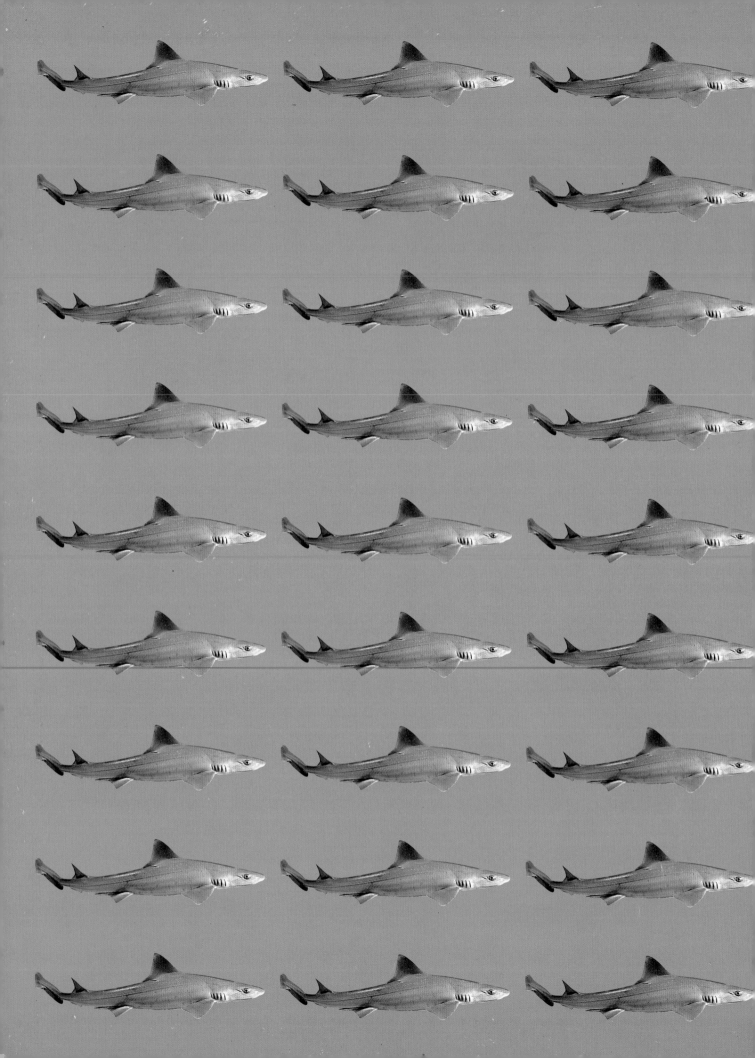